THE GREATEST OF THESE IS LOVE

1 Corinthians

NELSON

IMPACT™

Bible Study Series

THE
GREATEST OF
THESE IS LOVE

1 Corinthians

NELSON IMPACT
A Division of Thomas Nelson Publishers
Since 1798

www.thomasnelson.com

Published by Nelson Impact, a Division of Thomas Nelson, Inc., P.O. Box 141000, Nashville, Tennessee, 37214.

Scripture quotations marked (NKJV) are taken from *The Holy Bible,* The New King James Version®. Copyright © 1979, 1980, 1982, Thomas Nelson, Inc. Publishers.

ISBN 1-4185-0619-2

Printed in the United States of America.

06 07 08 EB 9 8 7 6 5 4 3 2 1

A Word from the Publisher…

Be diligent to present yourself approved to God, a worker who does not need to be ashamed, rightly dividing the word of truth.

2 Timothy 2:15 NKJV

We are so glad that you have chosen this study guide to enrich your biblical knowledge and strengthen your walk with God. Inside you will find great information that will deepen your understanding and knowledge of this book of the Bible.

Many tools are included to aid you in your study, including ancient and present-day maps of the Middle East, as well as timelines and charts to help you understand when the book was written and why. You will also benefit from sidebars placed strategically throughout this study guide, designed to give you expanded knowledge of language, theology, culture, and other details regarding the Scripture being studied.

We consider it a joy and a ministry to serve you and teach you through these study guides. May your heart be blessed, your mind expanded, and your spirit lifted as you walk through God's Word.

Blessings,

Edward (Les) Middleton, M. Div.
Editor-in-Chief, Nelson Impact

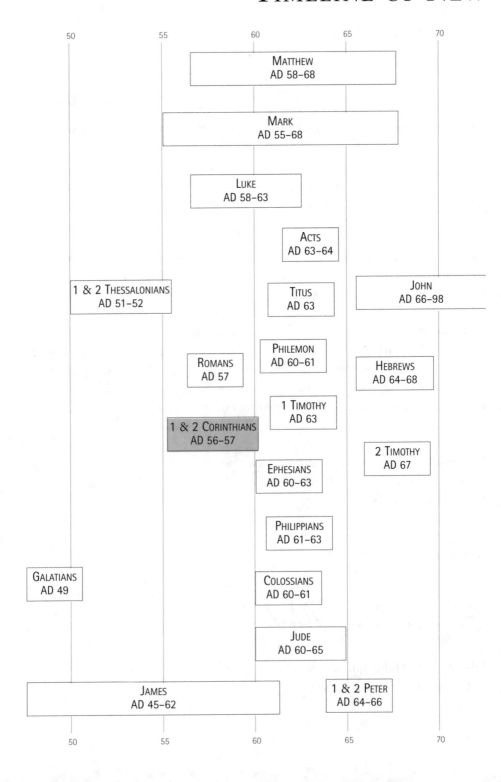

Testament Writings

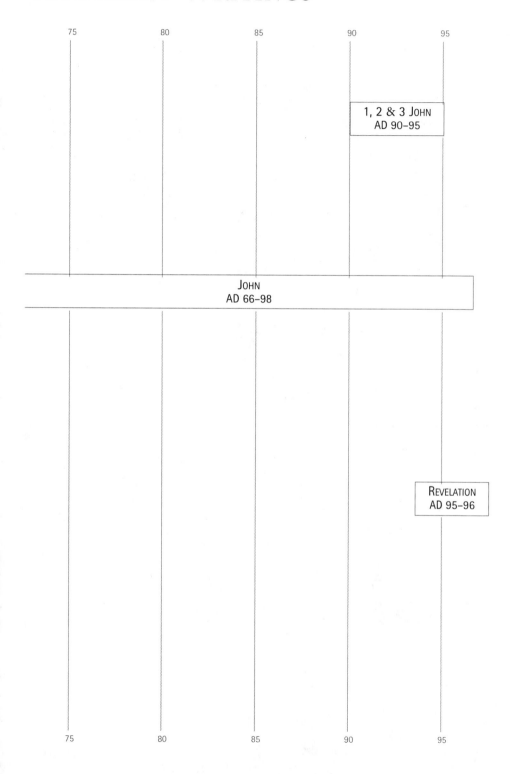

| 75 | 80 | 85 | 90 | 95 |

1, 2 & 3 John
AD 90–95

John
AD 66–98

Revelation
AD 95–96

OLD MIDDLE EAST

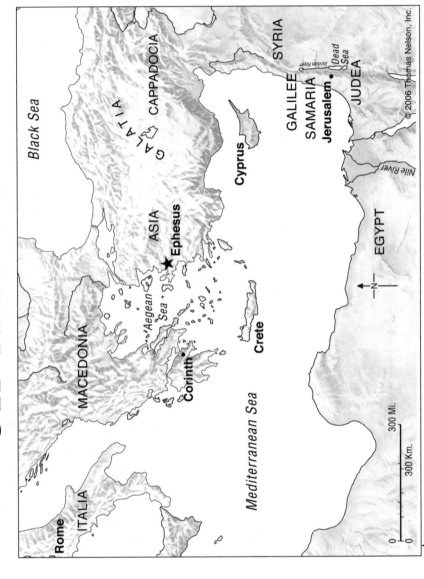

★ The book of 1 Corinthians was written in Ephesus.

© 2006 Thomas Nelson, Inc.

MIDDLE EAST OF TODAY

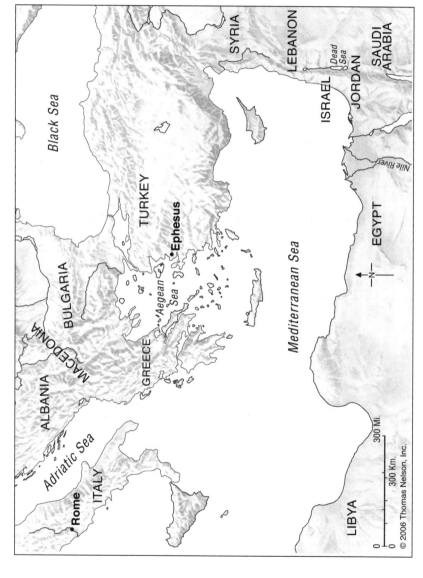

© 2006 Thomas Nelson, Inc.

OLD TESTAMENT DIVISIONS

The Pentateuch
Genesis
Exodus
Leviticus
Numbers
Deuteronomy

Wisdom Literature
Job
Psalms
Proverbs
Ecclesiastes
Song of Solomon

The Historical Books
Joshua
Judges
Ruth
1 Samuel
2 Samuel
1 Kings
2 Kings
1 Chronicles
2 Chronicles
Ezra
Nehemiah
Esther

The Prophetic Books
Isaiah
Jeremiah
Lamentations
Ezekiel
Daniel
Hosea
Joel
Amos
Obadiah
Jonah
Micah
Nahum
Habakkuk
Zephaniah
Haggai
Zechariah
Malachi

New Testament Divisions

The Four Gospels
Matthew
Mark
Luke
John

History
Acts

The Epistles of Paul
Romans
1 Corinthians
2 Corinthians
Galatians
Ephesians
Philippians
Colossians
1 Thessalonians
2 Thessalonians
1 Timothy
2 Timothy
Titus
Philemon

The General Epistles
Hebrews
James
1 Peter
2 Peter
1 John
2 John
3 John
Jude

Apocalyptic Literature
Revelation

ICON KEY

Throughout this study guide, you will find many icon sidebars that will aid and enrich your study of this book of the Bible. To help you identify what these icons represent, please refer to the key below.

BIBLICAL GRAB BAG

A biblical grab bag full of interesting facts and tidbits.

BIBLE

Further exploration of biblical principles and interpretations, along with a little food for thought.

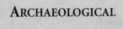

LANGUAGE

Word usages, definitions, interpretations, and information on the Greek and Hebrew languages.

CULTURE

Customs, traditions, and lifestyle practices in biblical times.

ARCHAEOLOGICAL

Archaeological discoveries and artifacts that relate to biblical life, as well as modern-day discoveries.

CONTENTS

Introduction   1

1   Salutation and Thanksgiving   9
    (1:1–9)

2   Division in the Church   15
    (1:10–4:21)

3   Disorders in the Church   29
    (5:1–6:20)

4   Instruction on Marriage   39
    (7:1–40)

5   Instruction on Christian Rights   51
    and Freedoms (8:1–11:1)

6   Instruction on Public Worship   63
    (11:2–34)

7   Instruction on Spiritual Gifts   71
    (12:1–14:40)

8   Instruction on the Resurrection   85
    (15:1–58)

9   Conclusion   95
     (16:1–24)

10   Coming to a Close   101

     How to Build Your Reference Library 103

INTRODUCTION

A ny struggling Christian today, or any troubled church congregation, would do well to begin a study of the New Testament book of 1 Corinthians. No other book of the Bible offers such a complete inventory of the problems that can plague the body of Christ—including immaturity, instability, divisiveness, jealousy, envy, legal conflicts, marital strife, sexual immorality, and misuse of spiritual gifts. More important, no other book offers such concise, practical, and scripturally sound solutions to these problems.

First Corinthians is one of the many letters written by the apostle Paul to members of the early Christian church. In a later message to the Romans, he wrote, "Do not be conformed to this world" (Rom. 12:2). He might just as easily have been addressing the citizens of Corinth, for in the first century the general population and members of the church there were very much influenced by the world. Located on a narrow isthmus between the Greek mainland and the peninsula known as Peloponnesus,

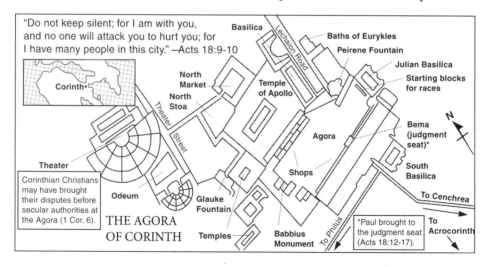

"Do not keep silent; for I am with you, and no one will attack you to hurt you; for I have many people in this city." —Acts 18:9-10

Basilica
Baths of Eurykles
Peirene Fountain
Julian Basilica
Starting blocks for races
Corinth
North Market
North Stoa
Temple of Apollo
Lechaion Road
Theater Street
Agora
Bema (judgment seat)*
Theater
South Basilica
Corinthian Christians may have brought their disputes before secular authorities at the Agora (1 Cor. 6).
Odeum
Glauke Fountain
Shops
To Cenchrea
THE AGORA OF CORINTH
Temples
Babbius Monument
*Paul brought to the judgment seat (Acts 18:12-17).
To Acrocorinth

Corinth was an ideal hub for commerce between Italy and Asia. Visitors from many parts of the globe brought a steady stream of new ideas and philosophies to the city of more than six hundred thousand people.

Some of these ideas were more beneficial than others. One of the most destructive consequences for a population that embraced a cosmopolitan atmosphere was a full-scale slide into decadence. During Paul's time, in fact, the city was infamous for its immorality. Greek plays of the day depicted Corinthians as drunkards and degenerates. At the temple dedicated to Aphrodite, goddess of love, worshipers practiced religious prostitution with as many as one thousand "sacred" priestesses. So widely known was the depravity of Corinth that the Greek verb "to Corinthianize" came to mean "to practice sexual immorality."

It was in this environment that Paul established a Christian church among Gentiles in Corinth during his second missionary journey (c. AD 49–52). Perhaps it was no surprise that troubles surfaced soon after. While in Ephesus on his third missionary journey (c. AD 53–57), Paul received a letter describing divisions and immorality in the church at Corinth. Believers were following individual Christian leaders rather than Christ Himself. They also were taking each other to court to settle disputes. Paul wrote 1 Corinthians in response to this news, as well as to answer questions about marriage, singleness, and Christian freedoms that arose in a second letter from Corinthian believers.

A CHANGED MAN

In some ways, Paul probably seemed an unlikely candidate to take on the decadence and spiritual apathy of Corinth. His appearance was apparently unremarkable. One second-century document described him as "a man of little stature, partly bald, with crooked legs, of vigorous physique, with eyes set close together and nose somewhat hooked."

SAUL BECOMES PAUL

The man we have come to know as the apostle Paul was given the name Saul at his birth. He grew up in Tarsus, the capital city of Cilicia in the eastern region of Asia Minor, where he acquired the skill of tent making. As a young man, he dedicated his energy to persecuting Jews who accepted the teaching of Jesus Christ.

That all changed when Saul met the Lord on his way to Damascus. According to tradition, God gave Saul the Hellenistic name Paul at the time of his conversion. The Scriptures, however, do not specify exactly when or why Saul became known as Paul. At the time of his first missionary journey, it appears he went by either name (Acts 13:19). After this time, however, at least in Scripture, he is referred to only as Paul.

The Hebrew name Saul means "asked (of God)," while the Roman Paul (Paulus in Latin) stands for "little." It was customary at the time to have both a given or birth name and a later new designation. It is possible that Scripture sticks mostly with the Greek name Paul because he focused the majority of his preaching and teaching on the Gentiles.

Furthermore, Paul was of Jewish ancestry, declaring himself a descendent of the tribe of Benjamin and a member of the strictest Jewish sect, the Pharisees (Phil. 3:5). Finally, to his profound regret later in life, Paul spent years of his life persecuting the followers of Jesus Christ (Acts 8:3). These were hardly credentials that would have earned the attention of newly converted Gentile believers!

But as we know, Paul's life changed forever when he encountered Jesus on the road to Damascus (Acts 9:5–6). After his conversion to the Christian faith, Paul dedicated the rest of his days to taking the message of Christ to the world. He embarked on four multiyear missionary journeys, beginning about AD 46 from Antioch and ending approximately sixteen years later in Rome.

During his second journey, Paul traveled with a coworker named Silas to Corinth, where he met two believers named Aquila and Priscilla. They ran a tent-making business, which would have been familiar to Paul. He stayed with them and preached every Sabbath to the Jews and Greeks. The Jews, however, rejected Paul and his teaching, so after that time he focused on the Gentiles (Acts 18:6).

One evening the Lord spoke to Paul in a vision, saying, "Do not be afraid, but speak, and do not keep silent; for I am with you, and no one will attack you to hurt you; for I have many people in this city" (Acts 18:9–10). Though the Jews attempted to have Paul arrested by the Romans, their efforts failed, and Paul stayed in Corinth for a year and a half before completing his second journey. Many Corinthians heard his preaching, believed, and were baptized.

WRITING ON THE ROAD

Virtually all New Testament scholars agree that the apostle known as Paul is the author of 1 Corinthians. Both the letter itself (1 Cor. 1:1–2; 16:21) and early church fathers acknowledge Paul as the writer. One of these early leaders was Clement of Rome, a coworker with Paul at Philippi (Phil. 4:3), who confirmed Paul's authorship in AD 96.

It appears that Paul wrote 1 Corinthians during his third missionary journey near the close of his three-year stay (Acts 20:31) in Ephesus. He refers to his plan to remain in Ephesus until Pentecost (1 Cor. 16:8), indicating that he intended to stay there less than a year. Paul probably wrote 1 Corinthians in AD 55 or 56. After leaving Ephesus and writing the letter that became known as 2 Corinthians, Paul visited Corinth a second time near the end of his third missionary journey.

PAUL ON THE ROAD TO DAMASCUS

Mediterranean Sea

Encounter with the resurrected Christ "near Damascus."

Damascus

GALILEE

Sea of Galilee

Caesarea

SAMARIA

Samaria

Jordan River

Jerusalem

Jericho

JUDEA

Dead Sea

—N—

0   40 Mi.
0   40 Km.

© 2006 Thomas Nelson, Inc.

AN APOSTLE'S INSTRUCTION

Paul begins his letter to the Corinthians with a salutation and an offering of thanks for God's grace. He then turns to the many problems facing believers in Corinth, beginning with divisions in the church. Paul shows that the Corinthians misunderstood the message of the Cross and the ministry of Christ. The root of their problems was pride, and the solution was to adopt a posture of humility.

Paul then addresses disorders in the church, including the failure to discipline an immoral brother, to resolve personal disputes in a godly manner, and to maintain sexual purity. In each case he provides the spiritual basis for reversing the failure.

Most of the rest of the book of 1 Corinthians deals with Paul's specific and practical instruction regarding six areas of concern. The first of these, a chapter on marriage, explores topics in

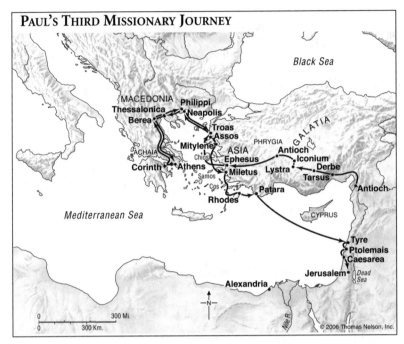

PAUL'S THIRD MISSIONARY JOURNEY

Black Sea

MACEDONIA
Philippi
Thessalonica
Neapolis
Berea
Troas
Assos
PHRYGIA
GALATIA
Mitylene
Chios
ASIA
Antioch
ACHAIA
Ephesus
Iconium
Corinth
Athens
Miletus
Lystra
Derbe
Samos
Tarsus
Cos
Patara
Antioch
Rhodes
CYPRUS

Mediterranean Sea

Tyre
Ptolemais
Caesarea
Jerusalem
Dead Sea
Alexandria

–N–

0   300 Mi.
0   300 Km.

Nile R.

© 2006 Thomas Nelson, Inc.

greater detail than previously covered in Scripture. These include the relationship between marriage and celibacy, divorce, and ministry, as well as a discussion of remarriage.

In the second area of concern, Paul makes a series of points about the rights and freedoms of believers, basing his points on a discussion of the practice of sacrificing food to idols. He shows how this practice relates to brotherly love, to his refusal to accept financial compensation from those who support the gospel, to discipline for the cause of Christ, and to temptation.

Paul offers instruction on public worship in the third area of concern before spending three chapters on the fourth area, a discussion of the unity and diversity of spiritual gifts and their place in worship. In the fifth area of concern, Paul provides a reaffirmation of the Christian faith and the bodily resurrection of Jesus, followed by answers to questions posed about the resurrection of the dead and the rapture of the living. A final chapter addresses the area of giving to the poor, followed by concluding exhortations and greetings.

First Corinthians includes some of the most well-known statements in the Bible. Within the section on spiritual gifts, Paul's treatise on love offers perhaps the best definition, and probably the most eloquent and frequently quoted text, regarding the subject that can be found in literature. The material on marriage and living as a single person has provided invaluable guidance to generation after generation. And near the end of his letter to the Corinthians, Paul includes the Bible's most detailed explanation of the resurrection of Christ and Christians.

PAUL'S LOST LETTER

First Corinthians is not the first letter that Paul wrote to the believers at the church of Corinth. In his rebuke of their failure to expel an immoral brother, Paul refers to a previous letter that instructed them to avoid sexually immoral people (1 Cor. 5:9).

Some scholars suggest that this earlier letter has been preserved in 2 Corinthians, believing that the latter is actually made up of parts of several letters. Most historians, however, pointing out that sexual immorality is addressed only briefly in 2 Corinthians (12:21), conclude that the earlier letter was simply lost, probably not long after it was received.

How This Study Guide Is Organized

Many methods are available for a close examination of the Bible, including a topical study of major subjects or a verse-by-verse analysis. As with other study guides in the Nelson Impact Bible Study Series, however, we have chosen the sequential approach. We will discuss the text in front-to-back order with our chapters divided by Paul's issue-by-issue instruction to the Corinthians.

We begin our study with an opening address and offer of thanks to God. This is followed by two chapters on divisions and disorders in the church. Then we explore Paul's teaching on marriage, Christian rights and freedoms, public worship, spiritual gifts, and the resurrection before concluding with a look at Paul's final comments.

As you investigate 1 Corinthians, try to read between the lines of Paul's stern words and detailed instruction. You will discover the heart of this beloved apostle: his hurt over the stumbles of his Christian brothers and sisters; his determination to follow Christ and spread His message regardless of any obstacles; and above all, his love for Jesus and His flock. The care and wisdom contained in these pages penned two thousand years ago may very well become a treasured guide to you for the rest of your days.

SALUTATION AND THANKSGIVING

1 CORINTHIANS 1:1–9

Before We Begin . . .

Since Christians are already saved by their faith, how important is it, in your view, for believers to show their allegiance to Christ by their actions?

Paul's letters have endured through the ages in part because of his skill as a word-smith. Even his initial greeting to the Corinthians is carefully constructed. In the first three verses, Paul introduces themes that will reappear in greater detail later in his text.

First Corinthians begins with a reminder of Paul's authority as a servant of God. In many ways, the entire letter feels like a disappointed father's stern but loving lecture to his children. It is appropriate, then, for Paul to open his remarks by reestablishing his position as an apostle carrying out the divine will of the Lord.

Fill in the blanks in the passage below, then answer the questions that follow.

Paul, called to be an _____ of Jesus Christ through the _____ of God, and Sosthenes our _____, To the _____ of God which is at _____, to those who are _____ in Christ Jesus, called to be _____, with all who in _____ place call on the name of Jesus Christ our _____, both theirs and ours. (1 Cor. 1:1–2 NKJV)

What gives Paul the authority to call himself an apostle of Christ (see Acts 9:5–6)?

Sosthenes probably recorded Paul's words on paper for him. He may have been the synagogue ruler publicly thrashed by the Jews as recorded in Acts 18:17. If so, what must have happened to bring him to the position of Paul's assistant?

By describing his readers as the "church of God," how is Paul subtly reminding the Corinthians of Him to whom they ultimately must answer for their actions?

Paul also says his readers are "sanctified in Christ Jesus"—in other words, set apart for the Lord. Have the Christian Corinthians demonstrated their standing before God in their behavior?

A SANCTIFIED READERSHIP

To sanctify means "to set apart for a sacred purpose." It can also mean "to make holy." Believers are sanctified by being declared holy through faith in Christ's atoning death on the cross or by being made holy through the work of the Holy Spirit in their lives. The former is sometimes called "positional" sanctification; the latter may be described as "progressive" sanctification.

Paul was unquestionably displeased by the reports he'd received on the conduct of the Corinthian believers. Even so, he described them as sanctified because of their relationship to Christ (positional sanctification). He hoped his letter would encourage the Corinthians to bring their actions in line with their position before God.

In verse 2, Paul emphasizes the unity of Christian believers in the phrase "with all who in every place call on the name of Jesus Christ." Why was this message so needed by the Corinthians?

Paul offers one of his typical greetings in verse 3 of 1 Corinthians 1. In many ways, the twin themes of grace and peace summarize his entire message. Grace is perhaps God's most significant gift to humanity, while peace is the result for all who turn over their minds and hearts to Him.

Read verse 3, then answer the questions below.

In what ways is Paul modeling grace to the Corinthians?

What does Paul imply about the deity and equality of God and Jesus by linking them here?

"I Thank My God Always"

In verse 4, it may seem strange for Paul to offer thanksgiving to God for the deeply troubled Corinthians. But a closer examination of this verse and those that follow reveals that Paul's praise is less for the Corinthians and more for the God who is working daily in the lives of Paul's readers:

> *I thank my God always concerning you for the grace of God which was given to you by Christ Jesus, that you were enriched in everything by Him in all utterance and all knowledge, even as the testimony of Christ was confirmed in you, so that you come short in no gift, eagerly waiting for the revelation of our Lord Jesus Christ, who will also confirm you to the end, that you may be blameless in the day of our Lord Jesus Christ. (1 Cor. 1:4–8 NKJV)*

What specific manifestations of grace in the lives of the Corinthians does Paul mention in this passage?

What spiritual gifts is Paul referring to in the phrase "all utterance and all knowledge" (v. 5 NKJV)?

How was possession of these gifts a testimony of Christ?

What makes Paul so confident that the sin-plagued Corinthians will stand blameless before God at the return of Christ?

Paul closes this section with a brief yet powerful statement about the faithfulness of God and the calling of believers. His use of the word *fellowship* highlights the unity that the Corinthians lacked and provides a smooth transition from the grace God offered in the past and will offer in the future to what Paul's readers must do in the present.

Read the following verse, then answer the questions below:

> God is faithful, by whom you were called into the fellowship of His Son, Jesus Christ our Lord. (1 Cor. 1:9 NKJV)

Paul demonstrates an unshakable confidence in the trustworthiness of God. How strong do you think the Corinthians' confidence was in the faithfulness of the Lord?

Do you believe it is possible to achieve genuine fellowship with the Creator of the universe? Why or why not?

esu

THE MEANING OF *FELLOWSHIP*

In the Greek language, the word for *fellowship* is *koinonia*, meaning "that which is shared in common." As used by Paul and other New Testament authors, the word signifies a believer's connection to the triune God—that is, one God coexisting in three separate yet equal parts: the Father, the Son, and the Holy Spirit.

During His ministry in the world, Jesus introduced the disciples to this concept of fellowship. They gained eternal life by their faith in Christ, and at their earthly deaths they entered into the fellowship. The unique fellowship begun in eternity between the Father and the Son was manifested through the incarnation of the Son, introduced to the disciples, and then through them extended to every believer through the indwelling of the Holy Spirit. When we enter into a genuine, heartfelt fellowship with other believers on earth, we gain the briefest glimpse into the wonderful, holy fellowship that awaits us in eternity.

PULLING IT ALL TOGETHER . . .

• Paul opens his remarks to the Corinthians by touching on several important themes: his authority as an apostle; his readers' status as "sanctified in Christ Jesus," that is, set apart for the Lord; the Corinthians' calling to be saints; and the unity that is theirs in Christ.

• By his emphasis on God's grace—he mentions it twice in the first four verses—Paul subtly reminds his audience that every blessing comes not from their own abilities but from God.

• Paul demonstrates the attitude the Corinthians should adopt by thanking God for them and for His work in their lives.

• The apostle concludes his introduction with a strong statement about the faithfulness of God and the calling of believers to fellowship.

DIVISION IN THE CHURCH

1 CORINTHIANS 1:10–4:21

Before We Begin . . .

Do you ever find yourself quarreling with others? What usually leads to the disagreement?

The first problem addressed by Paul in 1 Corinthians is division in the church. Apparently the Corinthians had begun to identify themselves with individual church leaders, placing their allegiance to men above their commitment to Christ. These wrong priorities led to quarrels among the believers.

What is particularly striking about these troubles in the early church is how relevant they are to us today. Christians still tend to place engaging and persuasive speakers, authors, and ministry leaders on a pedestal. Most of these men and women are genuine servants with hearts for the Lord—yet as we have seen all too often, even Christian leaders can fail publicly and spectacularly. No matter how spiritual or godly our ministry heroes seem to be, they are still imperfect human beings who fall short of the glory of the Lord.

Whenever we become too enamored of an individual believer, we run the risk of elevating that person above Jesus in our hearts and minds, just as the Corinthians did. Paul shows us that Christ alone is worthy of this kind of adoration. He is the only One who will never disappoint.

Read 1 Corinthians 1:10–17, then answer the following questions.

In verse 10, Paul makes his tenth reference to Christ in the first ten verses of 1 Corinthians. Why would he place so much emphasis on Jesus at the start of his letter?

Who are the four leaders Paul quotes the Corinthians as following?

1.

2.

3.

4.

Paul seems to find fault even with those who say, "I am of Christ" (v. 12 NKJV). How could those who followed Jesus also stir up dissension in the church?

Why does Paul say he was not sent to baptize? What does his statement seem to indicate about the emphasis the Corinthians put on those who performed the baptism ceremony?

WISDOM AND POWER

In this next section, Paul compares the wisdom of humanity to the wisdom and power of God. He shows that the Corinthians—and, of course, all Christians—must depend not on themselves, which will lead to destruction, but on the Lord.

In verse 19, Paul quotes from Isaiah 29:14, where God denounces the plan of the "wise" to seek an alliance with Egypt: "I will destroy the wisdom of the wise, and bring to nothing the understanding of the prudent" (1 Cor. 1:19 NKJV).

What does this verse say about God's attitude toward those who rely on their own wisdom?

Read 1 Corinthians 1:20–25, then answer the following questions.

In verse 20, "the wise" probably refers to a Greek philosopher; "the scribe" to a Jewish scholar trained to handle the Law; and "the disputer" to a Greek trained in rhetoric. All were professionals who attempted to solve problems through logic and debate. What does Paul say about the wisdom of this approach?

What are the two worldly viewpoints of the crucified Christ listed in verse 23?

1.

2.

What does Paul say about the "foolishness of God" in verse 25?

In verses 26–29, Paul draws out even more the contrast between the wisdom of the world and the wisdom of the Spirit. He also shows the prideful and arrogant Corinthians that without God they are merely foolish and weak.

Fill in the blanks below, then answer the questions that follow.

> *But God has chosen the _____ things of the world to put to shame the _____, and God has chosen the _____ things of the world to put to shame the things which are _____; and the _____ things of the world and the things which are _____ God has chosen, and the things which are not, to bring to _____ the things that are, that no _____ should glory in His presence. (1 Cor. 1:27–29 NKJV)*

By choosing the foolish, weak, base, and despised to reveal His truth, how does God ensure that He alone will receive the glory?

How is this approach consistent with the coming of a Messiah who in the eyes of the world is a lowly carpenter from Nazareth?

THE LOWLY SLAVE

In 1 Corinthians 1:28, Paul uses the words *base* and *despised* for things chosen by God, common terms at the time for the slave class. His readers likely would have understood that Paul was using slaves as a metaphor for people in low circumstances. Slaves in Corinth during the first century actually outnumbered the rest of the population. Of the 650,000 people in the city, as many as 400,000 were thought to be slaves.

In appearance, slaves were indistinguishable from their masters. One historian records that the senate once considered a proposal to require slaves to wear distinctive clothing. When someone pointed out that the slaves would then see their numbers advantage over the free population, however, the idea was quickly dropped.

In terms of lifestyle and social class, of course, slaves and their masters were at opposite ends of the spectrum. Many slave owners were thoughtless and cruel. Wives were known to take out their anger at their husbands by beating their slaves, a frequent enough occurrence that the city of Athens provided a temporary refuge for slaves to escape brutal treatment.

The lot of slaves gradually improved during the first century. Stoic philosophy taught that all persons were subject to fate and that slaves were not born inferior. The spread of Christianity also influenced some of the Romans to acknowledge the humanity of their slaves.

Read 1 Corinthians 1:30–31, then answer the following question.

According to verse 30, what four things did Jesus impart to humanity through His life and death on the cross?

1.

2.

3.

4.

Paul next addresses the futility of human wisdom by using his own ministry as an example. His preaching was unimpressive by human standards, yet through the power of the Spirit it moved the Corinthians to faith in Christ.

Read 1 Corinthians 2:1–5, then answer the following questions.

How does Paul describe his manner while preaching to the Corinthians (v. 3)?

How did Paul's lack of human persuasiveness become a demonstration of God's power?

SPIRITUAL WISDOM

Paul speaks here of a hidden wisdom available only to those who believe. Through the Holy Spirit, mysteries viewed as foolishness by the rest of the world are revealed to men and women of faith.

Read 1 Corinthians 2:6–8, then answer the following questions.

Who are the "mature" in verse 6?

What plan is at the heart of the "hidden" wisdom of God?

Read Paul's quote of Isaiah 64:4 below:

> *"Eye has not seen, nor ear heard,*
> *Nor have entered into the heart of man*
> *The things which God has prepared for those who love*
> *Him." (1 Cor. 2:9 NKJV)*

What things prepared by God is Paul referring to (see Eph.
1:3–14)?

In 1 Corinthians 2:10–16, Paul again emphasizes the contrast between the teachings of men and the teachings of the Holy Spirit, as well as humanity's dependence on the Spirit for knowledge and understanding. In the first four verses of chapter 3, Paul returns to his original theme in this section, dissension in the church, by pointing out that the Corinthian believers are still "babes in Christ" in terms of their spiritual maturity.

Read 1 Corinthians 2:10–3:4, then answer the questions below.

How is it possible for a believer to be both spiritual and carnal?

How does Paul express his disappointment with the Corinthians'
lack of spiritual growth?

SPIRITUAL JUDGMENT

When Paul says that "he who is spiritual judges all things" (1 Cor. 2:15 NKJV), he isn't telling us to show off our spiritual maturity by pronouncing judgments on every person and issue we run across. Rather, he wants us to realize that if we possess the Holy Spirit and are guided by Him, then we are able to apply spiritual discernment to the world around us.

In this section, Paul lists three types of people:
- Natural (1 Cor. 2:14)—those living without the Spirit
- Spiritual (1 Cor. 2:15)—those in whom the Spirit of God lives and produces growth
- Carnal (1 Cor. 3:1)—those who are believers but don't allow the Spirit to work in their lives

Paul saw the Corinthians as carnal—believers, but too immature to give the Holy Spirit a prominent place in their hearts. He urged them to move toward the spiritual and receive the full benefits and wisdom of the gift of the Holy Spirit (see Rom. 8:27).

MISUNDERSTANDING THE MINISTRY

In the first section of 1 Corinthians, Paul expressed his unhappiness with believers who had placed greater focus on church leaders than on Christ. Now he turns to the leaders themselves. Ministers in the church, after all, are servants accountable to God. Paul shows that in this role, they must be wary of cultivating the praise of men (as some of the Corinthians were apparently doing) rather than the approval of the Lord. Once again, Paul offers instruction that is just as valuable and needed today as it was two thousand years ago.

Read 1 Corinthians 3:5–16, then answer the following questions.

How does Paul discourage the idea of competition between leaders (vv. 5–7)?

What is the message to arrogant Corinthian ministers (v. 11)?

What can "wise builders" look forward to (v. 14)?

What is Paul's warning in verse 17?

Paul reemphasizes the foolishness of worldly wisdom in verses 18–20. He then makes a profound statement about "who belongs to whom" in the family of God.

Read 1 Corinthians 3:18–20, then fill in the blanks below and answer the questions that follow.

> *Therefore let no one _____ in men. For all things are _____: whether _____ or Apollos or Cephas, or the _____ or life or death, or things _____ or things to _____—all are yours. And you are _____, and Christ is _____. (1 Cor. 3:21–23 NKJV)*

How is it that Paul, Apollos, and Cephas (Peter) belong to Paul's Corinthian readers?

How can the world, life, death, and things present and future also belong to the Corinthians?

Who makes this possible?

What is Paul saying about the foolishness of competition between ministers?

Paul elevates the role of minister to a steward in 1 Corinthians 4:1. In Corinth, a steward would have been a slave who administered the affairs of his master's household. Paul is pointing out the important responsibility of ministers within God's church.

Read 1 Corinthians 4:1–5, then answer the questions below.

What is Paul saying about the importance of others' opinions in verse 3?

Who is the only One competent to judge others?

THE CURE FOR DIVISION

Paul concludes his teaching on division in the Corinthian church by identifying the central issue, a common problem throughout human history: pride. He then presents a practical solution, which is to imitate his own example.

Read 1 Corinthians 4:6–13, then answer the questions below.

What source is Paul referring to by "what is written" (v. 6)?

Does Paul really believe the Corinthians are rich, wise, and strong (vv. 8–10)? What is he saying to them?

What picture does Paul present of the life of service for Christ (vv. 11–13)? How does this picture contrast with what the Corinthians seemed to expect?

Paul's last words on the subject of division are both an assurance and a warning. He urges the Corinthian believers to follow his example:

> *I do not write these things to shame you, but as my beloved children I warn you. For though you might have ten thousand instructors in Christ, yet you do not have many fathers; for in Christ Jesus I have begotten you through the gospel. Therefore I urge you, imitate me.* (1 Cor. 4:14–16 NKJV)

Finally, Paul concludes this section with a promise to return soon, including a clear indication that he will deal with the Corinthians' transgressions in one manner or another.

Read 1 Corinthians 4:17–21, then answer the questions below.

What is Paul saying about his source of power for both teaching and discipline (v. 19)?

Though Paul is willing to do whatever is necessary to move the Corinthians closer to Christ, which option would he clearly prefer (v. 21)?

PULLING IT ALL TOGETHER . . .

• Paul opens this section with a discussion of divisions arising in the church because some believers are identifying themselves with individual leaders rather than as equal members of the body of Christ.

• A comparison of worldly wisdom with the wisdom and power of God shows that believers must shift their focus away from self and toward the Lord.

• We learn that the "hidden wisdom" of God is available only to believers who rely on the knowledge and guidance of the Holy Spirit.

• Like other believers, ministry leaders themselves are accountable to God. They must be wary of cultivating the praise of
others rather than the approval of the Lord.

• Paul identifies the root of the problem for division in the
church: pride. He urges the Corinthians to imitate his example and warns them of the consequences if they fail to change
their ways.

DISORDERS IN THE CHURCH

1 CORINTHIANS 5:1–6:20

Before We Begin . . .

How tolerant do you feel believers should be toward the sinful behavior of others?

After dealing with dissension among Corinthian believers, Paul turns his attention to disorders within the church. Three in particular are addressed: the Corinthians' failure to discipline an immoral brother; their inability to resolve personal disputes in a godly manner; and their lack of sexual purity. Many of the same problems highlighted in the previous section—pride and a dependence on human wisdom—are behind these new issues as well. And as noted before, these are problems that continue to plague us today.

In the first verses of chapter 5, Paul seems taken aback not just by a case of incest involving a Corinthian believer, but also by the astonishing lack of response by the rest of the church. The Corinthians apparently believed that because God's grace is limitless, their tolerance of sin also should be limitless.

Read 1 Corinthians 5:1–8, then answer the following questions.

What does Paul mean by the words "puffed up" in verse 2?

How might delivering a sinner to Satan save his spirit?

Even a pinch of leaven can contaminate an entire loaf of bread. What or who is the "old leaven" Paul refers to in verse 7?

UNLEAVENED DOUGH

When Paul wrote that "a little leaven leavens the whole lump" (1 Cor. 5:6), he was referring to the Feast of Unleavened Bread. The feast, closely linked with the Passover celebration, commemorated the first seven days of the Jews' exodus from Egypt. All leaven (or yeast) had to be removed from the house before the slaying of the Passover lamb, so the Passover meal itself included only unleavened bread.

In Scripture, leaven usually symbolizes evil or sin. In this section of his letter, Paul is calling on Corinthian believers to remove the leaven of sin because they are batches of unleavened dough—new creations in Christ.

In his previous letter to the Corinthians that apparently was lost, Paul instructed his readers to distance themselves from sexually immoral people. He wasn't talking about the pagans of Corinth, however, as the Corinthian believers incorrectly assumed. Rather, Paul wanted them to cut themselves off from immorality in their midst.

Read 1 Corinthians 5:9–11, then answer the questions below.

How would refusing to associate with unbelieving sinners contradict the instruction of Christ (see Matt. 28:19–20)?

What might have been Paul's reasons for commanding the Corinthians not to keep company or even eat with believers who were sexually immoral, covetous, idolaters, revilers, drunkards, or extortioners?

Fill in the blanks in the passage below, then answer the questions that follow.

> *For what have I _____ with _____ those*
> *also who are _____? Do you not judge those who*
> *are _____? But those who are outside*
> *_____ judges. Therefore "put _____ from*
> *yourselves the _____ person." (1 Cor. 5:12–13)*

Since Paul made no reference to disciplining the incestuous woman of verse 1, we can assume she was outside the church. Who would he say is responsible for her judgment?

How is Paul again calling on the Corinthians to use mature spiritual judgment?

What does he expect to be done with the immoral brother?

RESOLVING PERSONAL DISPUTES

The next section details Paul's instruction regarding personal disputes. The Corinthians seemed unable to resolve disagreements among themselves or even within the church, so they repeatedly brought lawsuits against Christian brothers in pagan courts—a practice that remains all too familiar today. Paul demonstrated little patience for the supposedly "wise" Corinthian believers who mocked Christianity with their public feuds.

Read 1 Corinthians 6:1–6, then answer the questions below.

Paul asks seven questions in the first five verses. Is he seeking information or trying to make a point (v. 5)?

Why does Paul seem especially concerned that lawsuits were brought before unbelievers (v. 6)?

In verses 7–8, Paul points out the futility of brothers taking each other to court and suggests a better approach. Read these two verses, then answer the questions below.

What kind of failure is Paul talking about in verse 7?

What does he say is a preferable response to a dispute?

How easy or hard is this approach for you?

Paul shows the Corinthians in verses 9–11 that they have been acting no differently than those without belief. Read the passage below, then answer the questions that follow.

> *Do you not know that the unrighteous will not inherit the kingdom of God? Do not be deceived. Neither fornicators, nor idolaters, nor adulterers, nor homosexuals, nor sodomites, nor thieves, nor covetous, nor drunkards, nor revilers, nor extortioners will inherit the kingdom of God. And such were some of you. But you were washed, but you were sanctified, but you were justified in the name of the Lord Jesus and by the Spirit of our God. (1 Cor. 6:9–11 NKJV)*

In what way were the Corinthians deceiving themselves?

What three words indicate that the Corinthians should have been living a new lifestyle?

1.

2.

3.

Homosexuality in the First Century

Paul's list of the unrighteous in 1 Corinthians 6:9–10 is similar to his earlier list (1 Cor. 5:11) and probably reflected the most common problems of the day. In the decadent Greco-Roman society of the first century, homosexuality would have been among the most prevalent problems.

For centuries the Greeks had exalted male homosexuality, in part because women were considered too simple to form an intellectual bond with a man. The Romans began imitating Greek culture in the second century BC, including homosexuality, though probably to a lesser degree than the Greeks. Fourteen of the first fifteen Roman emperors were thought to be homosexual or bisexual.

Paul made it clear, of course, in 1 Corinthians and in other letters preserved in the New Testament (Rom. 1:26–27; 1 Tim. 1:10) that he agreed with earlier Old Testament passages in Scripture denouncing homosexual relations as perverse and despicable in God's eyes (Lev. 18:22; 20:13). It was (and still is) sin that separated practitioners from God.

Sexual Purity

Paul shifts here from a discussion of personal disputes to the matter of maintaining sexual purity. He begins this section by quoting what are apparently two statements, or even slogans, made by one or more of the Corinthian believers: "All things are lawful for me" (1 Cor. 6:12) and "Foods for the stomach and the stomach for foods" (v. 13). Both display the attitude that believers are free to do whatever they please and that even sexual immorality will have no impact on their spiritual lives.

Read 1 Corinthians 6:12–14, then answer the following questions.

Paul seems to agree that the Corinthians are not bound by the ceremonial law of Moses. How can abuse of this freedom, however, be destructive?

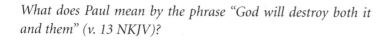

What does Paul mean by the phrase "God will destroy both it and them" (v. 13 NKJV)?

What is Paul saying about the value of our bodies in God's eyes (v. 13)?

Paul expands on his instruction about the dignity of our physical bodies in the next passage. The sexual union of a man and woman makes them "one flesh," a condition that should be reserved for marriage. A higher union even than the marriage bond is the believer's spiritual union with Christ.

Read 1 Corinthians 6:15–17, then answer the questions below.

What does Paul mean by the phrase "members of Christ" (v. 15 NKJV)?

How is our spiritual union with the Lord a model for marriage?

To conclude this section, Paul concisely describes what the Corinthians—and every believer—must do when confronted with sexual temptation.

Fill in the blanks below, then answer the questions that follow.

_____ sexual immorality. Every _____ that a man does is _____ the body, but he who commits sexual _____ sins against his _____ body. Or do you not know that your body is the _____ of the _____ _____ who is in you, whom you have from _____, and you are not your _____? For you were bought at a _____; therefore glorify God in your _____ and in your _____, which are God's. (1 Cor. 6:18–20 NKJV)

Why, rather than simply avoid or keep away from, does Paul command his readers to flee from sexual sin?

How can a person sin against his own body?

To whom do our bodies belong?

THE SACRED TEMPLE

The Greek word for "temple" used in 1 Corinthians 6:19 is *naos*, which refers to a temple building itself. The Greek *hieron*, on the other hand, indicates an entire temple complex. When Paul wrote, "Your body is the temple *[naos]* of the Holy Spirit," his readers most likely would have identified the word with a sacred place and understood that the presence of the Spirit would help them stand against the temptations of sexual immorality.

PULLING IT ALL TOGETHER . . .

• Chapter 5 of Paul's letter to the Corinthians records Paul's indignation not only at a case of incest involving an immoral brother but also of the attitude of the rest of the church toward the immorality. He instructs the Corinthians to stop glorying in their tolerant attitude, implement their spiritual judgment, and have no more to do with their immoral brother.

• Paul next condemns believers' practice of bringing lawsuits against one another in pagan courts. He tells them it would be preferable to suffer wrong and allow themselves to be cheated than to battle one another in court before unbelievers.

• Paul concludes his instruction on disorders in the church by demonstrating the seriousness of sexual immorality. He shows that the body is a temple of the Holy Spirit belonging to the Lord, and he commands believers to flee from sexual sin whenever temptation arises.

INSTRUCTION ON MARRIAGE

1 CORINTHIANS 7:1–40

Before We Begin ...

What would you say are the spiritual benefits—and potential spiritual drawbacks—of being married?

Paul originally learned of problems in the church at Corinth in a letter from the household of Chloe (1 Cor. 1:11), a respected woman who must have lived in either Corinth or Ephesus. The first six chapters of 1 Corinthians deal with these issues.

While Paul was in Ephesus, an official delegation from Corinth—Stephanas, Fortunatus, and Achaicus—personally delivered a second letter containing specific questions about issues such as marriage, singleness, and Christian liberty that were causing disagreements in the church (1 Cor. 16:17). Paul begins his response to these questions with the subject of marriage, providing wise counsel that could be considered required reading for every Christian couple even today.

The section begins with a discussion of celibacy and sexuality within marriage, with Paul praising the benefits of celibacy but also affirming God's gift of marriage: "It is good for a man not to touch a woman. Nevertheless, because of sexual immorality, let each man have his own wife, and let each woman have her own husband" (1 Cor. 7:1–2 NKJV).

Verse 1 seems to advocate celibacy and singleness. Why would Paul view this state as preferable to or at least equally desirable as marriage (see 1 Cor. 7:32–33)?

Why was Paul's advice in verse 2 especially appropriate in first-century Corinth?

Paul gives specific instruction to husbands and wives in verses 3–7. A close reading of the passage reveals one of the central teachings of Christ, a model for any successful marriage: "You shall love your neighbor [including your spouse!] as yourself" (Matt. 22:39 NKJV).

Read 1 Corinthians 7:3–7, then answer the questions below.

What is the emphasis of verses 3–4 on one's self or on one's partner?

Verse 5 states that both partners must agree to any abstention of sexual relations and that such an abstention should be temporary. Why is mutual consent important?

What does Paul say can happen if sexual relations are not resumed?

What spiritual activities should characterize a time of sexual abstention?

What gifts from God is Paul talking about in verse 7?

Once again, this time speaking specifically to the divorced and widowed, Paul upholds celibacy as a positive circumstance. At the same time, however, he again concludes that marriage is the better option for those who are filled with sexual passion.

Read 1 Corinthians 7:8–9, then answer the following questions.

According to these verses, how can a person know if he or she has the gift of celibacy?

How is Paul's instruction in verse 9 both biblical and practical?

MARRIAGE AND DIVORCE

Paul turns his attention to the issue of divorce and repeats the command of Christ: a wife and husband should not separate (see Mark 10:2–12). He also adds his own insights on believers who are married to unbelievers. This wisdom is offered through an apostle writing under the influence of the Holy Spirit (see 1 Cor. 7:40).

Fill in the blanks in the passage below, then answer the questions that follow.

> Now to the married I _____, yet not I but the
> _____: A wife is not to _____ from her
> husband. But even if she does depart, let her remain
> _____ or be _____ to her husband. And a
> husband is not to _____ his wife. (1 Cor. 7:10–11
> NKJV)

Paul states that a divorced wife should remain unmarried or reconcile with her husband. Does he mean this to apply to husbands also?

What does Paul want married couples on the brink of divorce to do? How can this be accomplished (see Eph. 4:31–32)?

Paul now addresses "the rest," that is, Christians married to unbelievers. We have no record of Jesus speaking to these issues, so it is the first testimony of the New Testament on this subject. Paul affirms that as a rule, even for a marriage between a believer and an unbeliever, divorce should be avoided. He does, however, provide for an exception: the unbeliever who insists on a divorce.

Read 1 Corinthians 7:10–16, then answer the following questions.

MARRIAGE, DIVORCE, AND REMARRIAGE IN CORINTH

Marriage in the Roman world in the first century had a very different connotation than what we understand today. It was generally treated more like a contract than a romantic relationship, often arranged by the fathers and not always with the bride's consent. The Roman groom was typically under age twenty-five at the time of his first marriage (Greek and Jewish men were likely to be a little older). Wives were generally much younger, usually marrying at the onset of puberty. It was rare for a first-time bride to be older than fifteen.

Divorce was easy under Roman law. Unlike Jewish law, which allowed only a husband to initiate a divorce, the Romans viewed marriage as a relationship of mutual consent. Either party could request and would be granted a divorce. A variety of factors—the lack of love in marriages treated more like business relationships, the frequency of infidelity, and the ability to obtain a divorce with little effort—led to rampant divorce and remarriage, especially among the higher Roman classes. Nearly every notable Roman in the centuries before and after Christ's birth divorced and remarried at least once.

The men and women of Corinth were certainly vulnerable to these influences that led to so many problems in the church. And, of course, many have drawn parallels between the fall of Rome, with its immoral society, and the immorality that plagues our modern world.

What reasons does Paul give for believers and unbelievers to stay together in marriage?

How might a believing spouse be a conduit for spiritual blessing on an unbelieving spouse and their children?

LIVE AS YOU ARE CALLED

Paul extends the principle of remaining in marriage to a person's general status in life. If someone becomes a believer, it's really not important whether or not that person is married, circumcised, or a slave. We can infer that the same applies to one's career or place of residence. Nothing is wrong with trying to improve one's station in life, but it is best to be content with current circumstances. What matters most is living according to the will of God.

Read 1 Corinthians 7:17–20, then answer the questions below.

What does this passage imply about the value and dignity of any kind of work or lifestyle so long as it is in keeping with Christ's teachings?

Why would new believers be tempted to make dramatic life changes?

Why would Paul say it is better to "remain in the same calling" (v. 20 NKJV)?

Paul points out one of the many paradoxes of Christianity in the passage below: the slave who turns over his life to the Lord gains freedom, yet the free man (as well as the slave) who becomes a believer is a slave for Christ.

Read the following passage, then answer the questions.

Were you called while a slave? Do not be concerned about it; but if you can be made free, rather use it. For he who is called in the Lord while a slave is the Lord's freedman. Likewise he who is called while free is Christ's slave. You were bought at a price; do not become slaves of men. Brethren, let each one remain with God in that state in which he was called. (1 Cor. 7:21–24 NKJV)

What kind of freedom do we gain through Christ?

What kind of slavery is Paul talking about in verse 22?

How does this kind of slavery differ from serving a human master?

VIRGINS AND WIDOWS

Once again, Paul applies the concept of continuing in one's calling, this time to the unmarried, particularly virgins and widows. He urges them to remain unmarried for three reasons: (1) the pressures against living a Christian life in decadent Corinth, (2) the anticipated imminent return of Christ, and (3) the opportunity for unencumbered service for the Lord.

Read 1 Corinthians 7:25–35, then answer the following questions.

In verse 29, the phrase "the time is short" may refer both to the anticipated return of Christ and to the brevity of earthly life. How does Paul urge believers to live in verses 29–31?

What does Paul mean when he says, "The form of this world is passing away" (v. 31 NKJV)?

Paul describes ways that the affairs of the world—including marriage—can distract a believer from serving God. Can you list other examples?

Scholars are somewhat divided in their interpretation of 1 Corinthians 7:36–38, a further commentary on marriage and virgins:

> *But if any man thinks he is behaving improperly toward his virgin, if she is past the flower of youth, and thus it must be, let him do what he wishes. He does not sin; let them marry. Nevertheless he who stands steadfast in his heart, having no necessity, but has power over his own will, and has so determined in his heart that he will keep his virgin, does well. So then he who gives her in marriage does well, but he who does not give her in marriage does better. (NKJV)*

WOMEN IN THE FIRST CENTURY

Paul's statement that married women must care about pleasing their husbands (1 Cor. 7:34) was certainly true, though perhaps not in the same sense that we would understand it today. Women of the first century were viewed by the male-dominated society as second-class citizens in need of education and tolerance. They were not included in census figures and had no voting rights.

Women were expected to carry out a wide range of tasks: cook, wash laundry, care for children, draw water, grind grain, make tents, host guests, make clothes, teach, and bury the dead, to name a few. Those in the upper classes, of course, had slaves to help with these activities. Female slaves were considered household property, including sexual property. Any children born by a female slave were legally considered the master's property.

It is also true, however, that under the Roman Empire women enjoyed greater social freedom than at any time before or since until modern times. Some ran businesses left to them when their husbands died and bought and sold property on their own. They were influential in social and political affairs, regularly ate and conversed with their husbands and guests, and by the end of the century took part in court cases and composed literary pieces.

Many modern scholars believe that "any man" in verse 36 refers to a prospective bridegroom. In this view, the fiancé may be having difficulty maintaining a celibate state with his bride-to-be. If such a man cannot control his sexual desires, it is permissible for them to marry sooner than originally intended.

Another interpretation is that Paul is speaking about a man who has refrained from marrying his fiancée because of hostility toward believers in Corinth. According to this view, Paul is saying that such a man who realizes his fiancée is growing past prime marriageable age may go ahead and marry her.

Other scholars, however, reject both of these interpretations, believing that "any man" refers to a virgin's father. They point out that the Greek word *gamizō* that appears in the original translation of this passage usually means "give in marriage," which supports the idea of a father as "any man." In this view, a father may have decided that his daughter should not marry, without understanding that she does not possess the gift of celibacy. Paul is then suggesting that such a father not feel obligated to abide by his decision. He is free to allow his daughter to marry. On the other hand, if the three conditions listed in verse 37 were met, he would do well not to give her in marriage.

Regardless of which interpretation is correct, the thrust of Paul's message remains the same: the unmarried should stay that way if they can manage it—but if not, it is perfectly acceptable for them to marry.

Paul's final comments in this section on remarriage and widows are consistent with everything stated before.

Read 1 Corinthians 7:39–40, then answer the questions below.

What is the one condition Paul placed on a widow seeking remarriage?

What does Paul mean when he says he has "the Spirit of God"?

PULLING IT ALL TOGETHER . . .

• Paul begins answering questions from the Corinthian church with a discussion of celibacy and marriage. He praises the benefits of celibacy but also affirms God's gift of marriage.

• Paul repeats Jesus' instruction that husbands and wives should not divorce. The only exception he mentions is a married unbeliever who wants a divorce from a believing spouse.

• The principle of remaining in marriage, Paul says, also applies to other parts of a person's life. What matters most is not improving one's station but living according to the will of God.

• The unmarried, including virgins and widows, should remain so—though it is permissible to marry if sexual self-control is not possible.

Instruction on Christian Rights and Freedoms

1 Corinthians 8:1–11:1

Before We Begin . . .

How would you describe your "rights" as a citizen? What about as a Christian?

Can you imagine any reasons to deny yourself these rights?

One of the questions brought to Ephesus by Stephanas, Fortunatus, and Achaicus was about the propriety of eating the meat of an animal offered in a pagan sacrifice. Paul's response here is extensive, indicating that he observed a deeper problem needing his attention, most likely the Corinthians' tendency toward self-centeredness.

In first-century Corinth, the meat for sale at a marketplace usually included portions that had been offered to a pagan god. In pagan ceremonies, part of a sacrifice was supposedly taken by a god, with the remainder to be eaten by the priests. Anything left over was sold in the marketplace. Without realizing it, a Christian might buy and eat meat offered to a false god. The Corinthians wanted to know if they were free to eat such meat.

Paul puts the question into perspective by instructing the Corinthians to consider the effect of their actions on others. It is less a question about what is permissible than a question about what demonstrates brotherly love. Christians have many freedoms but also a responsibility not to abuse those freedoms.

Read 1 Corinthians 8:1–6, then answer the questions below.

What does Paul say about those who believe they possess great knowledge?

Where should our knowledge of God lead us?

Since idols are nothing, what is Paul saying about eating meat offered to pagan gods?

In the next section, Paul clarifies that in itself, the act of eating the "pagan" meat is harmless. But he also points out the more important issue, which is that eating such meat could cause harm to others.

Read 1 Corinthians 8:7–8, then answer the following questions.

What knowledge is Paul referring to in verse 7?

What does Paul say about the impact of what we eat on our relationship with God?

Verses 9–13 spell out the danger of eating food offered to pagan gods. Paul sums up his instruction to the Corinthians on this matter in verse 9, a statement that can apply not just to food but to all Christian behavior: "But beware lest somehow this liberty of yours become a stumbling block to those who are weak" (1 Cor. 8:9 NKJV).

Read 1 Corinthians 8:9–13, then answer the questions that follow.

What example does Paul use to make his point in verse 10?

Against whom does a brother sin if he makes his weak brother stumble?

What does Paul say he would do to avoid such sin?

REGULATING PRIVILEGE

Perhaps sensing that some of the Corinthians by this point in the letter would be chafing at his instruction, Paul opens the next section with a renewed affirmation of his position as an apostle. He then illustrates the point of the previous chapter by relating it to his own life. Though he had the right as a Christian and an apostle, Paul did not eat and drink all that was available to him, he did not take a wife, and he refused to accept financial support from those to whom he ministered. He put his service to the Lord above personal desires.

Fill in the blanks in the passage below, then answer the questions that follow.

Am I not an _____? Am I not _____?
Have I not seen _____ _____ our Lord?
Are you not my _____ in the Lord? If I am not an
apostle to _____, yet doubtless I am to
_____. For you are the _____ of my
_____ in the Lord. (1 Cor. 9:1–2 NKJV)

What two arguments does Paul use to support his authority as an apostle?

1.

2.

Which of the two could the Corinthians have verified with their own eyes?

Paul next asserts his rights as a Christian minister and his reasons for not exercising those rights. Though he refuses any monetary gain for his ministry, he receives two rewards: his boast that he offers the gospel free of charge and the opportunity to see the gospel at work among those to whom he preaches.

Read 1 Corinthians 9:3–18, then answer the questions that follow.

What examples does Paul use to support his point about his rights as a Christian?

Why does Paul surrender these rights (v. 12)?

What is Paul's Scriptural basis for his statement in verse 14 (see Luke 10:7)?

What would Paul prefer to do rather than lose his "boast" or reward for spreading the message of the gospel?

A WINNING STRATEGY

In the next four verses, Paul explains his strategy for taking the gospel to unbelievers, both Jews living under the Law of Moses and Gentiles who are not.

Read 1 Corinthians 9:19–23, then answer the questions below.

Though Paul is not under the Law of the Old Testament, whose law does he submit to (v. 21)?

Though Paul is willing to conform to local customs in order to more easily spread the gospel, would he violate a commandment of God for this cause?

Paul next explains his attitude toward his mission and earthly life. The discipline and wholehearted commitment required are similar to the approach of an elite athlete. Paul expects nothing less than victory: "Do you not know that those who run in a race all run, but one receives the prize? Run in such a way that you may obtain it" (1 Cor. 9:24 NKJV).

Read the rest of chapter 9, then answer the following questions.

What is the difference between the prize an athlete competes for and the crown Paul aims to win?

What well-calculated methods does Paul use to win the "race" of living the Christian life?

THE GAMES OF GREECE

When Paul used the analogy of a competitive runner to show how seriously he took his ministry, he knew his audience would understand his point. Corinth was only seventy-five miles from Olympia, site of the famous Olympic Games. At the time of Paul's letter, the games had been held there every fourth year for more than eight centuries. Event winners earned great fame, a crown of laurel leaves, and perhaps a stipend of money from the city.

Corinth was also the host of the Isthmian Games, another important athletic festival held every other year. Competitors in these games endured ten months of mandatory training. Anyone who failed to complete the training was declared ineligible for the games themselves. The feature event of the Isthmian Games was an endurance race after which the winner received a pine wreath crown.

One of Paul's lessons was that the rewards for winning athletic events were inconsequential and fleeting, while the reward for living according to the will of God is eternal.

WARNINGS FROM HISTORY

Like Paul and the Corinthians, the Israelites were in the "race" to live a life that was pleasing to God. They were greatly blessed by God, yet they failed to please Him and were severely disciplined. Paul wanted the Corinthians to realize that even though they, too, were blessed, if they were reckless with the gifts God had granted, they also would face His holy wrath.

Fill in the blanks in the following passage.

*Moreover, brethren, I do not want you to be
_____ that all our _____ were under the
cloud, all _____ through the sea, all were
_____ into Moses in the _____ and in the
sea, all _____ the same spiritual food, and all
_____ the same spiritual drink. For they drank of
that spiritual _____ that followed them, and that
Rock was _____. But with most of them God was
_____ well pleased, for their _____ were
scattered in the wilderness. (1 Cor. 10:1–5 NKJV)*

Read 1 Corinthians 10:6–13, then answer the questions below.

*What are the five examples to avoid that Paul lists in verses
6–11?*

1.

2.

3.

4.

5.

*What does verse 12 seem to imply about the attitude of the
Corinthians?*

THE GOLDEN CALF

In 1 Corinthians 10:7, Paul refers to one of the most shameful incidents in the history of the Israelites. After God revealed His commandments to Moses on Mount Sinai, Moses informed the people of Israel (Exod. 24:3), then returned to the mountain. During the forty days Moses was gone, the people rejected God's commandments and convinced Aaron to construct an idol: a golden calf. They sacrificed burnt offerings before the calf, ate and drank and danced, and worshiped their man-made god.

God's reaction was swift. He sent Moses down from the mountain. Moses destroyed the calf, called the people of God to him, and set them against the rest; about three thousand Israelites were killed in one day by their brothers.

Paul wanted the Corinthians to recognize the human tendency to turn away from God, and he wanted them to understand the consequences that can result from such flagrant disobedience.

Paul reveals one of the important truths of Scripture in verse 13. For the Corinthians then and for us today, it is both a comfort and a warning. We will never face a temptation so overwhelming that we are powerless to resist. At the same time, we have no excuse for indulging in sin. God provides a way out of temptation; we can avoid sin if only we will look for the path to freedom.

> *No temptation has overtaken you except such as is common to man; but God is faithful, who will not allow you to be tempted beyond what you are able, but with the temptation will also make the way of escape, that you may be able to bear it. (1 Cor. 10:13 NKJV)*

DEALING WITH IDOLATRY

Paul takes one of his examples of Israel's failure before God, idolatry, and explains in greater detail just how the Corinthians should behave when confronted with it.

Read 1 Corinthians 10:14–30, then answer the questions below.

Even though an idol is nothing, what harm is done in participating in idol worship?

What core principle does Paul repeat in verses 23–24 (see 1 Cor. 6:12)?

What is equally practical, spiritual, and loving about Paul's instruction in verses 27–30?

Paul summarizes his point in this section, and in many ways he sums up what should be the daily goal of every Christian in 1 Corinthians 10:31–33. Notice that he also provides simple but profound advice for achieving this goal in 1 Corinthians 11:1.

> *Therefore, whether you eat or drink, or whatever you do, do all to the glory of God. Give no offense, either to the Jews or to the Greeks or to the church of God, just as I also please all men in all things, not seeking my own profit, but the profit of many, that they may be saved. Imitate me, just as I also imitate Christ. (1 Cor. 10:31–11:1 NKJV)*

PULLING IT ALL TOGETHER . . .

• For the first time in 1 Corinthians, Paul begins addressing the specific questions delivered to him by Stephanas, Fortunatus, and Achaicus. Paul answers that the Corinthians are indeed free to eat meat previously offered to pagan gods but that the more important matter is whether their actions will cause harm to other, less knowledgeable believers.

• Paul affirms his position as an apostle and his rights as a Christian, then explains that he does not exercise his rights because he puts service to the Lord above his personal desires.

• By conforming to the customs of the people around him, Paul was more easily able to communicate the gospel message. He approached this mission as an elite athlete would approach a race, with commitment and discipline that will lead to victory.

• The Israelites were greatly blessed by God, but they displeased Him through their recklessness and disobedience and were severely disciplined. Paul warns the Corinthians that the same fate awaits them unless they live according to God's will.

• Paul explains that every believer can overcome temptation by seeking the escape provided by God.

• Paul provides specific instruction on how to deal with idolatry, and he concludes this section by teaching that all activity should bring glory to God.

6

INSTRUCTION ON PUBLIC WORSHIP

1 CORINTHIANS 11:2–34

Before We Begin . . .

What is the significance of the Lord's Supper in your spiritual life?

Paul extends his theme of Christian rights and the impact of one's freedoms on others in the next section of 1 Corinthians. He deals here with the state of women in worship and the behavior of believers at the Lord's Supper. Once again, Paul addresses the Corinthians' tendencies toward self-centeredness. He emphasizes the importance of glorifying God and demonstrating an attitude of love toward one's Christian brothers and sisters.

After so many rebukes, Paul begins by praising the Corinthians for keeping certain traditions as he had taught. He then presents the Scriptural foundation for his newest instruction: "But I want you to know that the head of every man is Christ, the head of woman is man, and the head of Christ is God" (1 Cor. 11:3 NKJV).

"Head" in this case means spiritual authority, with God as the ultimate authority over all. It does not apply inferiority, as Christ is clearly not inferior to God. Some scholars believe that "head" also refers to origin or source, but others dispute this interpretation. In any case, Paul stresses in subsequent verses the importance of demonstrating respect for God's system of spiritual authority.

Read 1 Corinthians 11:2–9, then answer the questions that follow.

Why does Paul say a man's head should be uncovered during prayer?

Why does he say a woman's head should be covered?

In verses 8–9, what does Paul mean by "woman from man" (see Gen. 2:21) and "woman for the man" (see Gen. 2:20)?

TO COVER OR NOT TO COVER

At the time of Paul's letter to the Corinthians, the accepted social custom was for women to cover their hair during public worship. Women of the lower class in most of the Mediterranean world covered their heads. In the far eastern Mediterranean, conservative women even veiled their faces; in most other places, women wore a shawl over their hair.

Some women in Corinth, however—particularly those of the upper class—preferred to display their hairstyles and often left their heads uncovered. Women of both the upper class and the lower class would have attended Corinthian worship services together, no doubt leading to the conflict in question.

Paul takes care in verses 11–12 to specify that though men have spiritual authority over women, men need women just as women need men, and both must depend on the Lord. All that they have and are is from God.

Read 1 Corinthians 11:10–16, then answer the questions that follow.

What does Paul seem to be saying about the importance of appearances in verse 10, and how does it relate to his previous statements about a believer's rights?

In verses 14–15, is Paul teaching that men should have short hair and women long, or merely that this is one respectful way to display their differences?

CONDUCT AT THE LORD'S SUPPER

Paul now turns his attention to the conduct of the Corinthians at the Lord's Supper. The tone of his commentary here is particularly harsh. What apparently concerns Paul is that the Corinthians seem to have turned what should be a holy gathering marked by love for Christ and fellow Christians into an event centered on self-indulgence.

Fill in the blanks in the passage below, then answer the questions that follow.

Now in giving these instructions I do not _____ you, since you come together not for the _____ but for the _____. For first of all, when you come together as a _____, I hear that there are _____ among you, and in part I believe it. For there must also be _____ among you, that those who are _____ may be recognized among you. Therefore when you come together in one _____, it is not to eat the _____ _____. For in eating, each one takes his own _____ ahead of others; and one is _____ and another is _____. What! Do you not have _____ to eat and drink in? Or do you _____ the church of

God and _____ those who have nothing? What shall I _____ to you? Shall I _____ you in this? I do not praise you. (1 Cor. 11:17–22 NKJV)

How did the Corinthians come together "for the worse" (v. 17 NKJV)?

What specific complaints does Paul have about the way the Corinthians were behaving at the Lord's Supper?

What was the result of the Corinthians' actions (v. 22)?

In contrast to the Corinthians' selfish and reckless gatherings, Paul reminds them of what they already know—the true purpose of the Lord's Supper, the centerpiece of early Christian worship:

For I received from the Lord that which I also delivered to you: that the Lord Jesus on the same night in which He was betrayed took bread; and when He had given thanks, He broke it and said, "Take, eat; this is My body which is broken for you; do this in remembrance of Me." In the same manner He also took the cup after supper, saying, "This cup is the new covenant in My blood. This do, as often as you drink it, in remembrance of Me." For as often as you eat this bread and drink this cup, you proclaim the Lord's death till He comes. (1 Cor. 11:23–26 NKJV)

At the Lord's Supper, what does the bread symbolize?

What does the wine symbolize?

As quoted by Paul in verse 25, what did Jesus ask all believers to do at the Lord's Supper?

A NEW COVENANT

In 1 Corinthians 11:25, Paul quotes Jesus' words from Luke 22:20: "This cup is the new covenant in My blood." God made several covenants with people in the Old Testament. Among these were agreements with Adam and Eve (Gen. 3:15), Noah (Gen. 8:21–22; 2 Pet. 3:7, 15), Abraham (Gen. 12:1–3), Israel (Deut. 29:1–30:20), and David (2 Sam. 7:12–16; 22:51).

The new covenant that Jesus spoke of was another matter, however. Through the prophet Jeremiah, God promised to establish a new relationship with His people. Through His Son, He would write His law on human hearts: "I will put My law in their minds, and write it on their hearts; and I will be their God, and they shall be My people" (Jer. 31:33).

The new covenant is based on Christ's sacrifice on the cross. By faith, the sins of humanity are removed and forgotten. This is why Paul was so offended by the behavior of the Corinthians at the Lord's Supper. Whenever Christians gather for this holy occasion, they should remember the Lord's sacrifice and the fulfilled promise of God.

EXAMINATION TIME

In the next six verses of chapter 11, Paul teaches how the Corinthians should approach the Lord's Supper.

Read 1 Corinthians 11:27–32, then answer the questions below.

What should a believer do at the Lord's Supper (v. 28)?

What happens to the believer who, like the Corinthians, attends the Lord's Supper in an "unworthy manner"?

What happens to believers unwilling to judge themselves?

Paul concludes his teaching on the Lord's Supper with practical instructions for the Corinthians: "Therefore, my brethren, when you come together to eat, wait for one another. But if anyone is hungry, let him eat at home, lest you come together for judgment. And the rest I will set in order when I come" (1 Cor. 11:33–34 NKJV).

PULLING IT ALL TOGETHER . . .

• Paul again discusses Christian freedoms and the way that believers' actions affect others. He focuses in 1 Corinthians 11 on the state of women in worship and the conduct of believers at the Lord's Supper.

• As a sign of respect for the spiritual authority of men (which is granted by God), Paul teaches that women should cover their heads when praying or prophesying.

• Paul commands the Corinthians to stop their selfish and reckless behavior at the Lord's Supper and instead examine themselves to avoid the judgment of God.

INSTRUCTION ON SPIRITUAL GIFTS

1 CORINTHIANS 12:1–14:40

Before We Begin . . .

What is your understanding of the purpose of spiritual gifts?

As in other areas of their spiritual lives, the Corinthians also struggled with how to exercise their spiritual gifts appropriately. Their self-indulgent attitude toward this issue had led to disunity and chaos during worship.

Paul responds to these problems by again pointing out that love for others must be the first concern of the Corinthians. He begins this section by relating the nature and purpose of spiritual gifts, continues by giving an eloquent description and definition of love, and concludes by showing that love must regulate the exercise of spiritual gifts.

One of the interesting themes of 1 Corinthians 12 is the relationship between the unity of the body of Christ and the diversity of spiritual gifts. Paul shows that even though God may bless each of us with a unique gift, we remain one valuable part of the entire body.

Read 1 Corinthians 12:1–11, then answer the questions that follow.

Where can believers find diversity, and where can they find unity (vv. 4–6)?

Who benefits from the use of spiritual gifts?

What are the nine gifts listed by Paul that are granted through the Spirit? Which of these, if any, applies to you?

1.

2.

3.

4.

5.

6.

7.

8.

9.

SPIRITUAL GIFTS

The ministry of spiritual gifts originates in the New Testament. As described by Paul, a spiritual gift is a manifestation of the Holy Spirit that allows believers to minister to one another as part of the body of Christ. Each one is a gift of God's grace.

The New Testament lists at least twenty-one spiritual gifts that are imparted for the benefit of the church (see Rom. 12:3–7; 1 Cor. 12:1–12, 28; Eph. 4:11). They can be broken into three categories:

1. Ministry: apostle, evangelist, pastor, prophet, teacher
2. Motivational: administration, exhortation, giving, leadership, mercy, service
3. Charismatic: discernment, faith, healing, interpretation, knowledge, miracles, prophecy, tongues, wisdom

The allocation of spiritual gifts is the responsibility of the Holy Spirit. As believers, our job—once we discover what gifts we have—is to use them wisely and with loving consideration for our brothers and sisters in Christ.

In verse 12, Paul offers a three-part summary of his theme for 1 Corinthians 12: "For as the body is one and has many members, but all the members of that one body, being many, are one body, so also is Christ" (1 Cor. 12:12 NKJV).

Paul uses the illustration of a physical human body to drive home the interdependent relationship between individual members of the body of Christ and the body as a whole. It's hard to imagine a foot deciding to go its own way (even if it could think, talk, and walk on its own!). Yet that is what many Christians do when they set themselves apart from other believers. We all have roles to play as parts of the same "body"—the family of God.

Read 1 Corinthians 12:13–26, then answer the following questions.

What do these verses say about the value of each member of the body of Christ?

What should be the attitude of those with "greater" gifts?

What should be the attitude of believers toward those with "lesser" gifts?

How should believers demonstrate unity in the body (vv. 25–26)?

By "ranking" with numbers the spiritual gifts of apostles, prophets, and teachers in verse 28, Paul appears to be correcting a belief among the Corinthians that these were lesser gifts than, say, speaking in tongues. These three may be among the most valuable spiritual gifts of all since they benefit the entire body of Christ.

Read 1 Corinthians 12:27–31, then answer the following questions.

Who appoints spiritual gifts to believers (see vv. 18, 24, 28)? Why would Paul place such emphasis on this point?

What two spiritual gifts does Paul list last? Why might they be at the bottom of his list?

In verse 31, Paul hints at something even more valuable than spiritual gifts. What is it?

THE GREATEST GIFT

Some have described the thirteenth chapter of Paul's letter to the Corinthians as a "hymn to love," and for good reason. It is among the most moving and expressive passages, not only in Paul's letters, but in all of Scripture and literature.

Some scholars believe Paul composed this section at a previous time and inserted it here because it applied so well to the circumstances. Since the message of brotherly love is so prevalent throughout 1 Corinthians, however, it is just as likely that he penned it for the first time in Ephesus as he was addressing the believers in Corinth.

The chapter is divided into three parts:
1. The ineffectiveness of spiritual gifts without the fruit of the Spirit, which is love
2. The character of love
3. The contrast of the impermanence of gifts with the eternal quality of love

Read 1 Corinthians 13:1–3, then answer the following questions.

What does Paul say is the effect of speaking in tongues if not motivated by love?

What is the overall effect on both the giver and the receiver of spiritual gifts if love is not present?

What does this imply about the relationship between Christianity and love in general?

Verses 4–7 contain what may be the best definition ever provided of love:

> *Love suffers long and is kind; love does not envy; love does not parade itself, is not puffed up; does not behave rudely, does not seek its own, is not provoked, thinks no evil; does not rejoice in iniquity, but rejoices in the truth; bears all things, believes all things, hopes all things, endures all things. (NKJV)*

List the positive actions that characterize love. How many of these are true of your attitude toward others?

List the negative actions that characterize love. How many of these are true of your attitude toward others?

How important was the concept of love for others to Jesus (see John 13:34–35)?

The third section of chapter 13 focuses on the temporary condition of spiritual gifts, which one day will no longer be needed, and the eternal nature of love.

Read 1 Corinthians 13:8–10, then answer the questions that follow.

The phrase "Whether there are prophecies, they will fail [kata-geo in Greek]" can literally be translated as "Prophesies will be stopped" (v. 8). When do you think that will happen?

Scholars believe the phrase "that which is perfect" in verse 10 may refer to the completion of the canon of New Testament Scripture, the death of a Christian, the maturity of the church, or the Second Coming of Christ. Which makes most sense to you?

Paul speaks of his own growing maturity in the last verses of chapter 13, implying that all believers go through a process of maturity that temporarily includes the use of spiritual gifts.

Fill in the blanks in the passage below, then answer the questions that follow.

When I was a child, I _____ as a child, I _____ as a child, I _____ as a child; but when I became a _____, I put away childish things. For now we see in a _____, dimly, but then _____ to _____. Now I know in _____, but then I shall _____ just as I also am _____. And now abide _____, _____, _____, these three; but the greatest of these is _____. (1 Cor. 13:11–13 NKJV)

What are the "childish things" that believers will one day put away?

Whom will we eventually see face to face?

What are the three essential and eternal qualities described by Paul in verse 13?

1.

2.

3.

"IN A MIRROR, DIMLY"

At the time of Paul's writing, mirrors were often made from bronze, an alloy of copper and tin. Corinth was known as having the highest-quality bronze in the Mediterranean region. Corinthian bronze was even used in the temple of Jerusalem. These bronze mirrors could be polished to a high luster but were susceptible to rust and tarnish. The Romans also had learned to make mirrors of glass, though these often showed a cloudy or distorted image.

Whether copper or glass, either works for Paul's analogy of a mirror reflecting a dim image (1 Cor. 13:12). The partial state of our current knowledge of God contrasts with the complete knowledge we will have at the coming of Christ. Only then we will have the wonderful opportunity to see Him "face to face."

PROPHECY AND TONGUES

In 1 Corinthians 14, Paul takes two examples of spiritual gifts—prophecy and tongues—to illustrate how love for others must guide their use. The obvious implication is that love should be the primary consideration behind the use of any spiritual gift—and even better, behind any action by believers.

Read 1 Corinthians 14:1–5, then answer the questions below.

Which gift does Paul value more, prophecy or tongues? Why?

Does Paul see any benefit at all to speaking in tongues? What adds value to the gift of tongues?

Here Paul provides further explanation of his instruction on the value and limits of the gift of tongues.

Read 1 Corinthians 14:6–12, then answer the questions that follow.

What are the four methods Paul used to speak to the Corinthians?

How could a Christian speaking in tongues be like a trumpet player calling fellow soldiers into battle?

How can Paul's emphasis on clear communication be extended to all Christians who seek to spread the gospel?

What is the message of verse 12, one of the central themes of this section?

Paul again stresses his teaching that speaking in tongues is much more beneficial if the words can be interpreted for everyone's gain.

Fill in the blanks in the passage below, then answer the questions that follow.

> *Therefore let him who speaks in a _____ pray that he may _____. For if I pray in a tongue, my _____ prays, but my _____ is unfruitful. What is the _____ then? I will pray with the spirit, and I will also pray with the _____. I will sing with the _____, and I will also sing with the _____. Otherwise, if you _____ with the spirit, how will he who occupies the place of the _____ say "Amen" at your giving of thanks, since he does not _____ what you say? For you indeed give _____ well, but the other is not _____. (1 Cor. 14:13–17 NKJV)*

What is the key word in this passage? (Hint: It appears twice in verse 15.)

Who is the "other" referred to in verse 17?

Paul summarizes his teaching in this section in verses 18–19. The gift of tongues is valuable, but the ability to minister to others is far more so: "I thank my God I speak with tongues more than you all; yet in the church I would rather speak five words with my understanding, that I may teach others also, than ten thousand words in a tongue" (1 Cor. 14:18–19 NKJV).

A SIGN TO UNBELIEVERS

Paul includes here a portion of Isaiah's prophecy against Israel (Isa. 28:11–12). Since the Israelites refused to hear the message of the prophets, Isaiah predicted that another message would come, one delivered in an unintelligible tongue. This message represented God's discipline: "In the law it is written: 'With men of other tongues and other lips I will speak to this people; and yet, for all that, they will not hear Me'" (1 Cor. 14:21 NKJV).

Read 1 Corinthians 14:20–25, then answer the following questions.

What does Paul mean by "in malice be babes, but in understanding be mature" (v. 20)?

What will the uninformed or unbelievers say about the Corinthians who all speak in tongues?

What will the uninformed or unbelievers do when confronted with prophecy?

ORDERLY WORSHIP

Paul concludes his teaching with specific instruction on how to maintain orderly worship. He includes guidelines designed to keep the use of tongues under control and yet enable God's Spirit to speak through this gift.

Read 1 Corinthians 14:26–33, then answer the questions below.

What principle does Paul again set forth in verse 26?

In verse 32, Paul seems to indicate that a believer with the gift of prophecy still has control over his or her gift. What is the message of this verse?

What is the source of peace in worship, and indeed in every aspect of life (v. 33)?

The statement "Let your women keep silent in the churches" (1 Cor. 14:34) has stirred considerable debate. Some scholars believe this verse means that all speaking is prohibited. Others argue that the phrase refers to speaking in tongues, while others say only disruptive talk is forbidden. Another view is that Paul means to restrain a feminist group in Corinth, while still another says the prohibition relates only to judging the prophets. As you might imagine, one could easily start an argument over interpretations of this passage—and in the process miss the entire point of Paul's teaching!

Whatever Paul's exact meaning here, it is clear that he intended for orderly and respectful worship to be the rule of the day.

CREATION OR CULTURE?

One reason that Paul's words in 1 Corinthians 14:34 can lead to heated discussion is the conflict that might be described as "creation versus culture." Some scholars, citing Paul's statement about the headship of a man in 1 Corinthians 11:3 and his reference to the order of creation in 1 Corinthians 11:8, maintain that a timeless order was established at creation. Women are to be in submission to their husbands both at home (see Eph. 5:22) and in the church (see also 1 Tim. 2:11–12).

Other scholars, however, believe that Paul's meaning should be viewed within the context of the culture. In this view, Paul's primary concern was that believers show respect for others, which naturally included consideration of accepted social practices. And as Paul stated elsewhere, there were times for women to speak in church (see 1 Cor. 11:5).

Paul may not have provided enough information for us to settle the matter conclusively, but he did give us plenty of instruction on how to conduct the debate.

In addition to silence, what attitude does Paul teach that women should adopt?

In what context does Paul say women should ask questions?

What are Paul's last words on the issue of prophecy and tongues?

PULLING IT ALL TOGETHER . . .

• The Corinthians' struggles with applying spiritual gifts had led to disunity and chaos during worship. Paul shows that though each believer may receive a unique spiritual gift from God, their gifts are to be used for the benefit of all.

• Paul appears to "rank" the spiritual gifts of apostles, prophets, and teachers as the most valued gifts in the church, contrary to what the Corinthians seemed to believe.

• Paul describes and defines love, implying its importance in the use of spiritual gifts and in every act of a Christian.

• Paul gives specific instruction on how best to employ the spiritual gifts of prophecy and tongues. He relates that the gift of tongues is valuable, but the ability to minister to others is even more so.

• Orderly worship is the theme of Paul's final teaching in this section. He includes guidelines for the use of speaking in tongues and instructs women to "keep silent in the churches" (1 Cor. 14:34 NKJV), though his exact meaning here is a matter of debate.

INSTRUCTION ON THE RESURRECTION

1 CORINTHIANS 15:1–58

Before We Begin ...

What first comes to your mind when you think about the resurrection of Jesus?

The reports Paul received about the unfortunate behavior of the Corinthians—such as divisiveness, selfishness, and sexual immorality—already indicated an inconsistent or weak faith. But Paul was also told that some in the church denied the resurrection of Christ entirely. Despite Paul's previous visit and teaching, they had abandoned even the basic tenets of Christianity.

In the face of these reports, Paul certainly saw the need for a strong response. He focuses the last major teaching of his letter to the Corinthians on a vigorous affirmation of the Resurrection. He divides his argument into four parts: history, logic, theology, and experience.

Following this thorough defense, Paul answers three expressed or implied questions: How are the dead raised? What is the nature of a resurrected body? and What about those who are not dead at the return of Christ?

REALITY OF THE RISEN CHRIST

HISTORY

Paul delivers the heart of the gospel message beginning with verse 3. Everything he teaches is based on this evidence.

Read 1 Corinthians 15:1–8, then answer the following questions.

What are the three parts of the central event involving Jesus Christ that form the foundation of all of Christianity (vv. 3–4)?

1.

2.

3.

How many people witnessed the risen Christ?

At the time of 1 Corinthians, how many of these witnesses were still alive and able to verify that Jesus had risen from the dead?

Who was the last apostle to see the risen Jesus?

In verse 9 we catch another glimpse of what may be the regret Paul feels over his persecution of believers as a younger man. Yet he immediately acknowledges God's grace (also implying forgiveness) and its results.

Read 1 Corinthians 15:9–11, then answer the questions below.

What does Paul call himself as a result of his past?

How does Paul compare his efforts to those of the other apostles?

What, in the end, is most important about the apostles' work (v. 11)?

LOGIC

Paul next addresses the belief among some Corinthians that no one could rise from the dead; he explores this belief to its logical conclusion.

Fill in the blanks in the passage below, then answer the questions that follow.

Now if Christ is preached that He has been _____ from the dead, how do some among you say that there is no _____ of the dead? But if there is no resurrection of the dead, then _____ is not risen. And if Christ is not risen, then our preaching is _____ and your _____ is also empty. Yes, and we are found _____ witnesses of God, because we have _____ of God that He raised up Christ, whom He did not raise up—if in fact the _____ do not rise. For if the dead do not rise, then Christ is not risen. And if Christ is not risen, your faith is _____; you are still in your _____! Then also those who have fallen asleep in Christ have _____. If in this life only we have hope in Christ, we are of all men the most _____. (1 Cor. 15:12–19 NKJV)

According to verses 14 and 17, what is the status of faith if Christ is not risen?

If Christ is not risen, what is the status of those believers who have died?

What does Paul say of himself and other believers if Christ is not risen?

"A RESURRECTION OF DEAD ONES"

In 1 Corinthians 15:12, Paul uses the Greek word *anastasis*, which literally means "resurrection out from among dead ones." The same verb form, which expresses the certainty of Christ's bodily resurrection, appears a total of seven times in this passage (vv. 4, 12–14, 16–17, 20).

A more general reference to the resurrection also appears in verses 12 and 13, as well as in verse 42. In Romans 1:4, Jesus' resurrection is referred to as "a resurrection of dead ones." The same language appears in 1 Corinthians 15:21, literally translated as "For since through a man death came, so also through a Man came a resurrection of dead persons." Taking these verses as a whole, there seems no doubt that Paul was indicating that eternal life is available to believers through the resurrection of Christ.

THEOLOGY

Paul shows that through the disobedience of one man, Adam, death came into the world—but through the obedience of a second man, Jesus, eternal life through resurrection is possible for all:

> *But now Christ is risen from the dead, and has become the firstfruits of those who have fallen asleep. For since by man came death, by Man also came the resurrection of the dead. For as in Adam all die, even so in Christ all shall be made alive. (1 Cor. 15:20–22 NKJV)*

What do you think Paul means by "firstfruits" in verse 20 (see Exod. 23:16, 19)?

Who are "those who have fallen asleep"?

Starting with verse 23, we see that God designed a specific order of events for the Resurrection. The last of these is the destruction of death and Christ's giving up His authority over heaven and earth to God.

Read 1 Corinthians 15:23–28, then answer the questions below.

What enemies might Paul be referring to in verse 25?

How do we know that Jesus has authority over "all things" (see Ps. 8:6; Matt. 22:44; 28:18)?

EXPERIENCE

To conclude his case for the reality of the Resurrection, Paul draws on the experience of the Corinthians and his own life. His dedication and love for people alone testified to his commitment to the cause of Christ.

Read 1 Corinthians 15:29–33, then answer the questions below.

How dangerous was Paul's work as an apostle?

In verse 32, what is the philosophy Paul proposes to follow if there is no Resurrection? Do you know people who live by this philosophy?

What is Paul advising Corinthian believers to do regarding those who deny the Resurrection?

BAPTISM OF THE DEAD

The phrase "baptized for the dead" in 1 Corinthians 15:29 has inspired scores of possible interpretations. Some of these include the following:

Living believers in Corinth, perhaps in keeping with previous pagan practices, were being baptized for believers who had died without baptism. This practice continues today among Mormons, who believe that the dead can be saved if someone living is baptized on their behalf. This concept conflicts, however, with Scripture and the requirement of faith (see Acts 16:30–31; Rom. 1:17; Heb. 9:27).

Corinthian believers were being baptized in anticipation of the resurrection of the dead.

New Christians were being baptized to "replace" the ranks of believers who had died.

Paul himself does not openly endorse or prohibit baptism of the dead in his letters, though by asking what "they" will do in 1 Corinthians 15:29, he clearly distinguishes it from his own practice and teaching. In any case, the reference is made almost in passing and in the context of the passage appears intended to support his message that such efforts, whether appropriate or not, are pointless if there is no risen Christ.

THE RESURRECTION BODY

Paul completes his discussion of the Resurrection by answering three questions. The first two, expressed in verse 35, pertain to the resurrection of the dead:

> *But someone will say, "How are the dead raised up? And with what body do they come?" Foolish one, what you sow is not made alive unless it dies. And what you sow,*

you do not sow that body that shall be, but mere grain—perhaps wheat or some other grain. But God gives it a body as He pleases, and to each seed its own body. (1 Cor. 15:35–38 NKJV)

How is belief in the Resurrection like belief in a seed that becomes a plant?

What does God do for each seed that grows in the ground—and by implication, for each believer who dies?

Read 1 Corinthians 15:39–49, then answer the questions below.

What contrasts between earthly bodies and heavenly bodies is Paul making (vv. 42–43)?

How does Paul describe the contrast (v. 44)?

What can we as believers look forward to (v. 49)?

RAPTURE OF THE LIVING

Paul's final words on the Resurrection answer the unexpressed question: What of those who are not dead at the return of Christ?

Read 1 Corinthians 15:50–55, then answer the questions below.

What will happen to living believers when Jesus comes again (v. 51)?

How quickly will this change take place?

Will death be able to touch these believers?

The last three verses of chapter 15 provide a final contrast between death and eternal life, followed by practical instruction so that the Corinthians would not lose their eternal reward:

> *The sting of death is sin, and the strength of sin is the law. But thanks be to God, who gives us the victory through our Lord Jesus Christ. Therefore, my beloved brethren, be steadfast, immovable, always abounding in the work of the Lord, knowing that your labor is not in vain in the Lord. (1 Cor. 15:56–58 NKJV)*

Pulling It All Together . . .

- Since Paul had received reports that some in the church denied the resurrection of Christ, the last major teaching of Paul's letter to the Corinthians begins with a vigorous affirmation of Jesus' resurrection.

- Paul presents his case from four perspectives: history, logic, theology, and experience.

- Paul asks and then answers a pair of questions: How are the dead raised? and What is the nature of a resurrected body?

- Chapter 15 of Paul's letter ends with an explanation of what happens to living believers at the second coming of Christ.

9

CONCLUSION

1 CORINTHIANS 16:1–24

Before We Begin ...

How many blessings can you think of that result from giving a portion of your income to God?

If you could summarize all of Paul's teaching in 1 Corinthians in a single statement, what would it be?

Paul's passion for Christ and his mission, as well as his extensive knowledge of theology and Scripture, are evident throughout 1 Corinthians—but so is his practical nature. Here, at the beginning of the last chapter of his letter, he provides instruction on one specific concern of the church, the needy of Jerusalem.

We also learn of Paul's personal plans for the future, as well as those of Timothy and Apollos. Before last greetings and a farewell, Paul includes final exhortations that in many ways summarize his message in all of 1 Corinthians. His words easily could serve as a motto for any believer today.

COLLECTION FOR THE POOR

The first four verses of chapter 16 concern a last question from the Corinthian delegation of Stephanas, Fortunatus, and Archaicus. It is interesting that Paul never uses the word *tithe* when discussing giving, even though he puts more emphasis on giving than any other New Testament author.

From several of Paul's writings, we learn that giving should be a regular practice, that it should be in proportion to a believer's income, and that everyone should contribute. We also see that Paul is scrupulous in money matters. He avoids solicitation for himself and prefers to let others handle gifts to the needy.

Read 1 Corinthians 16:1–4, then answer the questions below.

How often are believers expected to set aside money for God's purposes?

Why didn't Paul plan to take a collection upon his arrival in Corinth?

Why do you think he was so careful regarding matters of money?

The Joy of Giving

In 2 Corinthians, Paul provided an example of giving that may have revealed part of his motivation for urging the Corinthians to regularly set aside gifts for God. He wrote of Macedonian believers, who were extremely poor:

In a great trial of affliction the abundance of their joy and their deep poverty abounded in the riches of their liberality. For I bear witness that according to their ability, yes, and beyond their ability, they were freely willing, imploring us with much urgency that we would receive the gift and the fellowship of the ministering to the saints. (2 Cor. 8:2–4 NKJV)

Out of obedience and joy, the Macedonian believers gave far beyond what Paul expected or sought. Paul no doubt wanted the Corinthians also to experience the blessing of this kind of joy!

Plans for the Future

The next eight verses of chapter 16 concern Paul's plans regarding future visits, both by himself and his coworkers, Timothy and Apollos. One revealing passage, in terms of Paul's attitude and persistence, is contained in verses 8–9: "But I will tarry in Ephesus until Pentecost. For a great and effective door has opened to me, and there are many adversaries" (NKJV).

Read 1 Corinthians 16:5–12, then answer the following questions.

Where did Paul plan to go before reuniting with the Corinthians?

What does verse 9 say about Paul's determination in the face of opposition?

What do verses 10–11 indicate about Timothy's personality, as well as the general state of the Corinthian church?

LAST EXHORTATIONS

1 Corinthians 16:13–14 is a concise, inspiring exhortation, not only for the Corinthians but for all followers of Christ: "Watch, stand fast in the faith, be brave, be strong. Let all that you do be done with love" (NKJV).

Write out each point in this fivefold instruction, and add an example of how you can apply it to your own life:

1.

2.

3.

4.

5.

Read 1 Corinthians 16:15–18, then answer the following questions.

Whom does Paul commend for their devotion to ministry?

What effect did they have on Paul?

How does Paul expect the Corinthians to treat them?

FINAL GREETINGS

Paul ends his letter to the Corinthians with several final state-ments: greetings; instructions for them to give each other a "holy kiss"; a salutation in his own handwriting; a passionate warning, perhaps aimed at false teachers; and a plea for Christ to return.

THE HOLY KISS

The idea of a "holy kiss" (1 Cor. 16:20) appears several times in the New Testament (Rom. 16:16; 2 Cor. 13:12; 1 Thess. 5:25; 1 Pet. 5:14) and was intended as a symbol of love, forgiveness, and unity among believers. It was a com-mon way to begin the celebration of the Lord's Supper.

It appears that at the time of Paul's letter, the holy kiss was exchanged with members of both genders. Beginning in the late second century, following criticism from nonbelievers and consideration of the danger of erotic abuse, the suggestion arose to separate the sexes for the holy kiss. This new arrangement was apparently common practice by the third century. At the time of the early church, however, the holy kiss was seen as an appropriate expression of the bond between Christians.

Paul's last words return to one of his primary themes—love—expressed through his own example: "The grace of our Lord Jesus Christ be with you. My love be with you all in Christ Jesus. Amen" (1 Cor. 16:23–24 NKJV).

PULLING IT ALL TOGETHER . . .

• The first four verses of chapter 16 concern a last question from the delegation from Corinth about gifts for the saints. Paul instructs that gifts should be set aside and collected weekly.

• Paul tells of his plans for a future visit to the Corinthians, as well as visits by Timothy and Apollos.

• The Corinthians receive Paul's final exhortations, including an admonishment that everything be done in love.

• Paul sends his farewells to the believers at Corinth, ending with his wish for love to be with them all.

10 COMING TO A CLOSE

The letter from the apostle Paul now known as 1 Corinthians hardly portrays the Corinthian church in a flattering light. Too many believers there were sexually immoral, prone to disputes among themselves, self-indulgent, filled with pride, and willing to disregard even the most basic tenets of their faith. And that, we might be tempted to add, was on a good day!

Yet before we judge the Corinthians too harshly, we might compare their struggles to the church and our individual spiritual lives in the twenty-first century. In recent years, we, too, have seen our share of sex scandals, disputes, selfish schemes, prideful statements, and a general erosion of the foundations of faith. After a review of the headlines of our day, one could conclude that the church has made little progress in the last two thousand years.

First Corinthians, then, is much more than an indictment of an ancient and immature people who fell short of their potential as members of the body of Christ. It is a document that speaks to us right where we are, with wisdom that is just as relevant—if not more so—than it was in the first century AD.

One theme that emerges from Paul's writing is the need for spiritual maturity. The Corinthians were cavalier about their faith, sometimes going through the motions of Christian practice (such as the Lord's Supper) without considering its true impact and meaning. They seemed to have little concern for the consequences of their often immoral actions. Like the Israelites before them, they risked the wrath of God by their blatant disrespect for His will and blessings.

To counteract these tendencies, Paul urged the Corinthians to "draw a line in the sand." They were to flee immorality, cut off all contact with immoral brothers, put an end to lawsuits among brothers, and show respect for the Lord and each other during worship. Their focus was to be not on themselves but on the Father and Son—counsel that would serve us well today.

Perhaps the central message of 1 Corinthians, however, is the primacy of love in the heart and life of a Christian. Paul elevated love even above faith and hope: "the greatest of these is love" (1 Cor. 13:13). Spiritual gifts are a blessing from God, yet their use means little to the giver or receiver if not motivated by love. Every act, every relationship, and even every thought is to be grounded in the perfect love that comes from heaven.

Paul demonstrated this kind of love in his ministry to the Corinthians and to all people. Though the tone of his letter is often severe, the motivation behind it was one of caring. Paul's transformation from an unrelenting persecutor of Christians to a dedicated and loving apostle gives us hope for our own lives. If we open our eyes and hearts to Jesus, He can change us for eternity.

How to Build Your Reference Library

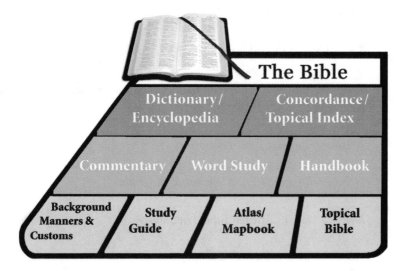

GREAT RESOURCES FOR BUILDING YOUR REFERENCE LIBRARY

DICTIONARIES AND ENCYCLOPEDIAS

All About the Bible: The Ultimate A-to-Z® Illustrated Guide to the Key People, Places, and Things

Every Man in the Bible by Larry Richards

Every Woman in the Bible by Larry Richards and Sue Richards

Nelson's Compact Bible Dictionary

Nelson's Illustrated Encyclopedia of the Bible

Nelson's New Illustrated Bible Dictionary

Nelson's Student Bible Dictionary

So That's What It Means! The Ultimate A-to-Z Resource by Don Campbell, Wendell Johnston, John Walvoord, and John Witmer

Vine's Complete Expository Dictionary of Old and New Testament Words by W. E. Vine and Merrill F. Unger

CONCORDANCES AND TOPICAL INDEXES

Nelson's Quick Reference Bible Concordance by Ronald F. Youngblood

The New Strong's Exhaustive Concordance of the Bible by James Strong

COMMENTARIES

Believer's Bible Commentary by William MacDonald

Matthew Henry's Concise Commentary on the Whole Bible by Matthew Henry

The MacArthur Bible Commentary by John MacArthur

Nelson's New Illustrated Bible Commentary

Thru the Bible series by J. Vernon McGee

HANDBOOKS

Nelson's Compact Bible Handbook

Nelson's Complete Book of Bible Maps and Charts

Nelson's Illustrated Bible Handbook

Nelson's New Illustrated Bible Manners and Customs by Howard F. Vos

With the Word: The Chapter-by-Chapter Bible Handbook by Warren W. Wiersbe

For more great resources, please visit *www.thomasnelson.com.*

NELSON IMPACT™ STUDY GUIDES

The Finest Study Bible EVER!

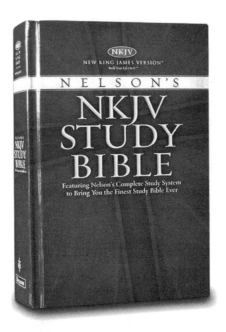

Nelson's NKJV Study Bible helps you understand, apply and grow in a life-long journey through God's Word.

NELSON IMPACT
A Division of Thomas Nelson Publishers
Since 1798

The Nelson Impact Team is here to answer your questions and suggestions as to how we can create more resources that benefit you, your family, and your community.

Contact us at Impact@thomasnelson.com